I0831084

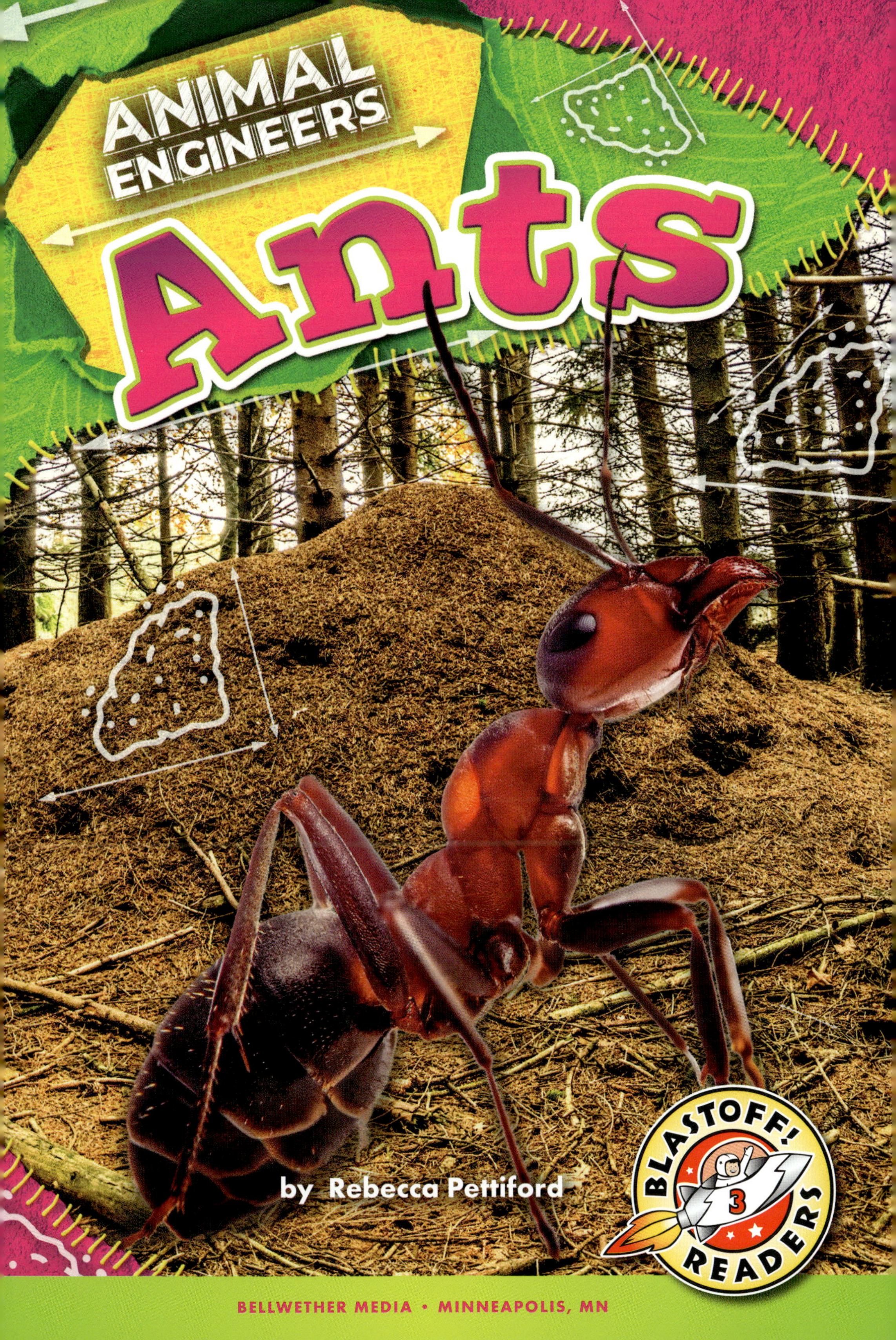
ANIMAL ENGINEERS
Ants
by Rebecca Pettiford
BLASTOFF! 3 READERS
BELLWETHER MEDIA • MINNEAPOLIS, MN

Blastoff! Readers are carefully developed by literacy experts to build reading stamina and move students toward fluency by combining standards-based content with developmentally appropriate text.

Level 1 provides the most support through repetition of high-frequency words, light text, predictable sentence patterns, and strong visual support.

Level 2 offers early readers a bit more challenge through varied sentences, increased text load, and text-supportive special features.

Level 3 advances early-fluent readers toward fluency through increased text load, less reliance on photos, advancing concepts, longer sentences, and more complex special features.

★ **Blastoff! Universe**

Reading Level

This edition first published in 2025 by Bellwether Media, Inc.

Library of Congress Cataloging-in-Publication Data

LC record for Ants available at: https://lccn.loc.gov/2024015044

Editor: Rachael Barnes Designer: Josh Brink

Printed in the United States of America, North Mankato, MN.

Table of Contents

Nest Builders

Ants are tiny, social **insects**. They live together in **colonies**.

Most ant colonies build nests. A nest houses ants, food, eggs, and **larvae**. It keeps ants safe from **predators**.

larvae

nest

Ants live almost everywhere on Earth. They often live in warm **habitats** where there is plenty of food.

Ant Range Map

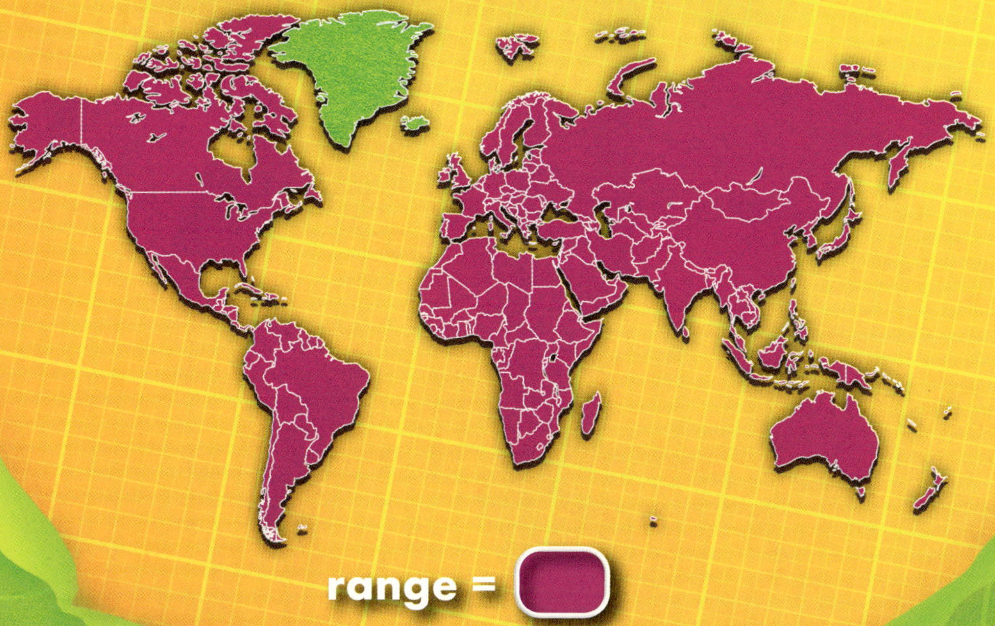

There are over 12,000 ant **species**! These insects are strong. Some move a lot of soil to build their homes.

Planning a Nest

queen ant

New ant colonies start when queen ants leave their old homes. Many find a **mate** in the spring.

Then queens search
for a safe place
to lay their eggs.

Queen ants nest in soil, wood, and plants. They look for **moist** areas with food nearby.

Building Materials

soil

wood

plants

They settle in and lay their eggs. Queens never leave the nest again unless their colony is in danger.

Time to Build!

Soon the eggs **hatch**. Most are small female ants. They become workers for the colony.

Many workers build the nest. They find food and care for young ants. Some **defend** the colony.

food

Workers use their **mandibles** to dig and carry objects out of the nest. Workers often remove dirt and rocks. They make many trips.

Workers place dirt near the nest entrances. Sometimes this forms anthills!

Ant nests have **chambers**. There are separate chambers for eggs, larvae, and food. The queen has her own chamber.

As the colony grows, workers dig more tunnels and chambers. The nest can take weeks or months to finish.

The Nest Is Ready!

long-lasting ant nest

Many nests support colonies as long as the queen is laying eggs. Some colonies and their nests last up to 30 years!

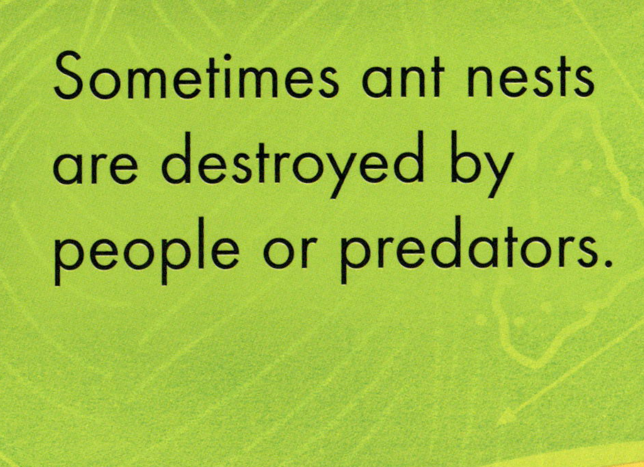

Sometimes ant nests are destroyed by people or predators.

predator

When a colony is large enough, the queen produces new queens and males.

Adult queens and males leave to find mates from other colonies. The queen ants start new nests!

Inside An Ant Nest

- chambers house the queen, eggs, food, and other ants
- tunnels connect chambers and lead to nest exits

chamber

exit

tunnel

Glossary

chambers—rooms in ant nests that are used for a special purpose

colonies—groups of ants; colonies live together in the same nest.

defend—to keep safe

habitats—the natural homes of plants and animals

hatch—to break open

insects—small animals with six legs and hard outer bodies; an insect's body is divided into three parts.

larvae—baby ants that have just hatched from eggs

mandibles—one of the two parts of the mouth on some insects; mandibles are often used for biting, chewing, cutting, and digging.

mate—one of a pair of adult animals that produce offspring

moist—slightly wet

predators—animals that hunt other animals for food

species—kinds of animals

To Learn More

AT THE LIBRARY

Levy, Janey. *Ants and Aphids.* New York, N.Y.: Gareth Stevens Publishing, 2022.

Lock, Deborah. *Ant Antics.* New York, N.Y.: DK Publishing, 2023.

Pettiford, Rebecca. *Honeybees.* Minneapolis, Minn.: Bellwether Media, 2025.

ON THE WEB

FACTSURFER

Factsurfer.com gives you a safe, fun way to find more information.

1. Go to www.factsurfer.com.
2. Enter "ants" into the search box and click 🔍.
3. Select your book cover to see a list of related content.

Index

The images in this book are reproduced through the courtesy of: Andrey Pavlov, cover (ant); rdp15, cover (anthill); Irina Kozorog, p. 3 (TOC); Henrik Larsson, p. 4 (ant larva); Azay photography, pp. 4-5; Eric Isselee, pp. 6-7, 15 (ant call out); Hartmut Goldhahn, p. 8; pokergecko, p. 9; Christian Ziegler/ Danita Delimon, Agent/ Alamy, pp. 10-11; Torychemistry, p. 11 (soil); Yongkiet Jitwattanatam, p. 11 (plants); Travis Wallace, p. 11 (wood); Bezuglaya Tatiana, p. 12 (worker); ervin herman, pp. 12-13; Pascal Guay, pp. 14-15; Naturefolio/ Alamy, pp. 16-17; Yunhyok Choi, p. 17; Kersti Lindstrom, p. 18; Martin Harvey/ Alamy, p. 19; Andi111, p. 20; Pavel Krasensky, p. 21 (chamber); Itsik Marom/ Alamy, p. 21 (exit); Grant Heilman Photography/ Alamy, p. 21 (tunnel); Nomadsoul1, pp. 20-21 (ant nest chambers); Sherjaca, pp. 20-21 (anthill top); Holger Kirk, p. 23.